# White Walls

## HERBERT WILLIAMS

INDEPENDENT INNOVATIVE INTERNATIONAL

Published by Cinnamon Press
Meirion House, Glan yr afon, Tanygrisiau
Blaenau Ffestiniog, Gwynedd, LL41 3SU
www.cinnamonpress.com
The right of Herbert Williams to be identified as author of this work has been asserted by him in accordance with the Copyright, Designs and Patent Act, 1988. Copyright © 2011 Herbert Williams.
ISBN: 978-1-907090-61-5

British Library Cataloguing in Publication Data. A CIP record for this book can be obtained from the British Library.

Designed and typeset in Palatino by Cinnamon Press.
Cover from original artwork – Long Corridor © agency dreamstime

Printed in Poland

Cinnamon Press is represented in the UK by Inpress Ltd www.inpressbooks.co.uk and in Wales by the Welsh Books Council www.cllc.org.uk.

The publisher acknowledges the support of the Welsh Books Council.

## Acknowledgements

Some of the poems in this collection first appeared in Sons of Camus International Journal, Envoi, Seventh Quarry, Poetry Nottingham, Planet, The Interpreter's House, Red Poets and Roundyhouse. My thanks to the editors concerned for their support of my work.

# Contents

## *For Dorothy*

*You're with me every day,*
*My honey, my roses,*
*Quiet as thought, breathing*
*Grace and forgiveness like prayer*

# White Walls

# White

White was the place they sent me to;
The walls were white, deathly white,
The women wore white and the men wore white,
And whiter than all, the ray machines.

And white was the paper they made me sign
To say the things I would undergo,
And white were the faces of those near death.

And when I left my thoughts were white;
My mind was white and my head was white,
And white was the shroud they were stitching for me,
And white were the songs they sang at my grave.

# Pain

Here?  Not quite.  To the right.
That it?  Up a bit.
How's this?  Ah, yes.

Her hands soft-press, caress,
easing emollient gel into my flesh.
An act of love that's free of love's duress.

# Mother Love

I told my wife I may have prostate cancer.
*Oh babe,* she cried, and put her arms around me.

# The Bond

A Robin Redbreast in a cage
puts all Heaven in a rage.
But does Heaven rage for aged men
trapped inside a regimen
of drugs to keep within control
the brittle bond of flesh and soul?

I see no reason why it should.
To break the bond is surely good.

# Self-knowledge

It's not infectious.
You don't catch it by
breathing, kissing,
mating, eating

or by
drinking piss
swimming sewers
stroking lepers.

It's part of you
that turns traitor,
a malfunction
inside.

So blame your
self
for cancer.
No one else.

# Cancer Hospital

white
walls

white
coats

white
machines

white
silence

white
healing

# Trapped

in my body
useless body
fit 4 fuckall

rescue me
queenofsheba
cleopatra
helenoftroy

arouse me
you bitches

# Killjoys

They're killing off my tes-
tosterone.  It is less
to them than Earl Grey tea,
balls of fluff beneath the bed.

*Hang on I say.  I am*
*a father five times over*
*and although*
*less lustful than I used to be*
*I've no desire*
*to be without desire*
*and have a wife*
*to be a husband to.*

*The cancer feeds*
*on your testosterone,*
*therefore the less the better,*
they explain.

And then they casually add,
*You'll have hot flushes*
*like menopausal women*
*perhaps put on some flesh across the chest.*

*You mean, have breasts?*
*What cup size will I need?*
*I have to know.*

They smile indulgently.
I don't smile back.

# Butterflies

I shall stay in my room, counting butterflies.
See how they come,
twitching their fingers like bats.
I look at them, admiring.  And they respond
with small, secret smiles.  I put those smiles

in a drawer when they're gone,
saving them for a brainy day
when thought presses down on my head.

# Edge of the World

On the edge of the world
on this far side of Wales
I watch the skies change.
Clouds bunch like fists,
then high, rippling,
or vague, like shadows of thought.
Sunsets abuse art,
impossible colours, bizarre effects.
Around me the sense
of the thinness of people;
their works puny, inept.

On the edge of the world
we know there is nothing
beyond.  Sun
drowns, night
comes.
*Requiescat in pace.*

# Road Map

I live in a small compass:
North, the shops.
West, the fields.
East, the city.
South, the river.

Magnetic north
default position.

Death.

# Spin

Moses, that old magician,
had it right, of course.
He laid it on the line.  Made ten
commandments.

The trouble is, interpreting
'Thou shalt not kill.' Did it mean
precisely that?  Or were there
exceptions?

He did not add, 'Except in war,'
or, 'When your life is threatened.'
Perhaps want of space
on tablets of stone
leaves no room for riders.

In time, one Jesus came along,
putting his own spin on it.
But no-one had much time for him.
Not even Christians.

# Paedo?

Mr Vaughan
as in porn

wheedling
needling

selling tea
from a little cart

smart

eyeing me
craftily

Mam chats away
I'm the prey

ten years old
Vaughan gets bold

*Goes to pictures,*
*does he?*

I freeze

Mam pours the teas

# Winter Morning

Ivy on fence
stirs in wind,
Makes rhythm, leaves
flapping like frail
drummers.

A heron slowly wings
from one side the window to the other.
My wife sees it, having
a gift for serendipity
I don't possess.

It's a short walk to shops but things
happen.  A man
speaks, a foetal stranger.
*I like a quiet Christmas.*
*Can't stand noise.  That's the true*
*meaning of Christmas.  Peace and quiet.*
I ponder this.

We live edgeways
to Cardiff.  A big field
off Birdie's Lane grows
men with dogs, boys
with fishing rods,
and myself.

Nothing more.

# Madam Death

She's far away, as far
as Jupiter and Mars,
so far one does not feel
the breath of her coming.

We know she's there but can
ignore her.  So much
to do.  The dross
of everyday existence.

She calls on friends.
We say
our last goodbyes.
She goes away.

And all the time
her visits get more frequent

and closer still
to home

until at last

# The Monk

*The body of a monk was found floating on a Burmese river in 2007,*
*after protests against the imposition of martial law*


The source of life
bears a strange burden.
It carries it reluctantly,
much preferring something
that fits its purpose.
A boat, perhaps, that it
sustains:
*I lift you, while I*
*yield to your wish, to claim*
*a little part of me.*

This man-that-was
gives nothing and can take
only the water's weight.
His robes are leaden with it.
He drowns in faith.

# Dead man walking

my father still walks
along the street, pace
measured, cloth-
capped (except on trilbied
Sunday), eyes
glazed with good
humour, greeting
neighbour and friend, *Good
morning/afternoon/evening* for
strangers, never a rough
word or ever a cutting cold
dead

the only one he does not see
is me, lurking
fifty years on, older than
he is, stranger in
time beyond his own,
far out of sight

# Crossing the bridge

I feel his presence still.
Is he trying to lure me over?
That means there is a bridge
for me to cross.

It was not always so.
He used to be the one
who crossed the bridge.
An only child
eager to join in.

So many of us!
One more – especially his –
was simply one more voice
to add to the cacophony.

Why should I cross the bridge?
What can he offer?
No, Emlyn, wait.
I am not ready.

He sighs, *The party's over*
*where you are.  Think about it.*
*Three of you there, that's all.*
*The rest are over here.*

I know I have to cross,
but not today.

He smiles.  He knows.

# being dead

howell rang tonight to say
he had said goodbye to the sea for you
you could not say goodbye yourself
being dead and having no voice

being dead and having no voice
you cannot say hello to me
not that you did very often
when you had the voice you have no longer

when you had the voice you have no longer
you said many things in younger days
and I said many things back to you
I can't say now and never will

what I can't say now and never will
is how I loved the sight of you
your length of face and depth of eye
the way you shook when excited

the way you shook when excited
your cheeks all a-quiver
oh you were a strange man
such a strange man my cousin

such a strange man my cousin
and now you are stranger
having become in a twinkling
a soul without body

a soul without body
so how can your cheeks quiver
and how can you speak to me
having no voice

having no voice
yet still I can hear you

# The Thinking Man's Future

A sensate being
but for how long
the crystal ball
is dark with doubt
the tea leaves hide
inside a bag
and Gypsy May
is pensioned off

If Time is fake
imagining
I may exist
before my birth
and read the runes
and brew the tea
the simple way
our grannies knew
and I will choose
not to be born
the words I write
will disappear

# The Common Lot

The common lot
is flushing out
by cancer, old age, suicide,
while life goes on, why should it not,
for all this is the common lot.

And we begin, as others do,
in childhood and simplicity,
but later comes duplicity,
and all such is the common lot.

And there is war and there is pain,
and there's the sad old question Why?
and all who ask it have to die,
for theirs is but the common lot.

And when we die, what then, what then?
Again, again, again, again.

# For Dorothy

I could praise
your joyousness, the way
you are a privilege about the house

And I could sing
your quietude
but you would say that makes you sound too dull

As a wife
you're comradeship for life

And you're a lover
though mother five times over

# Bricks

Churchill built
walls
laying brick on
brick
smoothing
cement with
calm, reflective eyes.

He made
pictures of
scenes he saw.
Brush poised, he
stared
hour after hour.

Hitler too
painted. They had
something in common.

It was bricks that
separated them.
Hitler built,
but only in the mind,

A Reich that would last
a thousand years!
It dazzled him.

Churchill could
destroy
as well as Hitler.

Building was
a different matter.

# Lightfoot, Heavyfoot

Lightfoot, I ran down-
stairs to get the mail.

Heavyfoot now, I trudge
down to make the tea.

# Ghosts

Ghosts hover around me
beseeching    bewailing
*Give me life! Give me life!*
How can I?   I am powerless.

Ghosts quiver around me
of friends long departed,
they shake in their fury
that I can do nothing

# Islands 1

Ideally, small.  With swaying palms.
Girls in grass skirts.  And music
of a certain kind.

If tiny and remote
they're desert islands.  Single
palm tree.  Castaway
or two (but never three).
Grist for cartoonist's
mill or radio programme.
*Time for another record.*
Sweetly said.

Places apart, by definition.
Away from it all –
wives, kids, bills, the mess
of living by the rulebook.

Of course, no man is one,
or woman either.  All connect.
Where then lies the essential strip of water?
In tolerance, perhaps.  And understanding.
Separate we stand.  Too conjoined, we fall.

# Islands 2

They are best imagined.  Tracts
of peace, perfection even,
where we can hide away
and be ourselves.

Finding them's the thing –
then getting there.
The locals look askance,
talking of tide-race
sandbanks, changing weather.

Trouble is, they're so seductive,
luring us out with siren voices.
Islands are other women –

and, like them, so ordinary
once you set fatal foot upon the shore.

# The Teacher

Taking some to task, and others
to his heart, he rides
the peaks and troughs of governance.
His nation is no easy one
to rule, with laws
set by a wide authority yet some
by him alone.  It is a mixed
and restless population.
Some yield to his command, others
question and rebel.  He needs
the finer points of judgment to succeed.

And who's the judge of that?
It takes a wiser counsel than his own.

# Après-midi

Surpassing all enlightenment, the will
tunnels us through black rocks of dissonance.
It is not enough to say
sorry afterwards.  The deed is done.
The harsh word, the crank
of worthless satisfaction, all make
the discord that will deafen us
in gaunt remembrance.  Nothing we do
will make amends.  God,
in his wisdom, knows this.
Faint not nor fear, the old hymn says.

But we do fear, and fainting
lacks the potential that it had
in days of sal volatile.  But still
the will persists.  Indulge it,
for it will slacken soon, the bark
of knowledge defer to
the feeble wrap of caution.

Age will repay you not with time
but with the lack of it,
the futile calculation
of what store remains -
time for this but not for that.
Who knows?
The final act is murder.

# Shocks to the System

can arise from most amazing things
e.g Ruskin whose
marriage was destroyed by pubic hair
(his bride's of course).  The sight of it
bushing the part of her that he'd imagined
would be as smooth and classical
as any in the paintings he admired
upset him so, he simply could not face her.
Poor Mrs R.  To be rejected thus
for false aestheticism is appalling.
Likewise (in kind if not degree)
the shock administered to H Macmillan
by young Pres Kennedy who told him
that if he went three days without a fuck
he had a headache.  Supermac
(whose wife was being regularly shagged
by Robert B, Conservative MP)
could only gravely nod
and turn the conversation to
the price of butter.

What else? The shock
of Galileo to the Pope of Rome?
A fine affair I know
to find the sun that always warmed
the Vatican did not go round the earth
as in all decency it should
but stood quite still
while Earth paid its respects
by driving people dizzy.

# Er Cof

Last night we unveiled
a plaque for John Tripp
in Whitchurch Public Library.

All of us were there.
Ifor and Gill,
Pete Finch,
Meic Stephens (of course),
Dai Smith, Sam Adams
and full supporting cast.

And Jean, sweet Jean,
faithful to John
to the last.

There was a poem or two.
A laugh or two.
A drink or two.

When we left
the lights went out.

The plaque remained
in the dark.

# road to ruin

stockpiles of arms
pillocks of leaders
dealers in death
breath of corruption
deception of people
ripple of scandal
vandals of earth
birth of distrust
lusting for power
hour of revenge
lunge to oblivion
thus Armageddon

# poppies

the call to arms
the boys join up
pals brigades
they stride to war

hiding fears
in khaki drill
uniform
their will to win

to france to france
excitedly
they picture luscious
mad moiselles

they learn the way
to strip a gun
they'd rather strip
a mad moiselle

the papers roar
the people shout
the pacifists
are drowned in piss

and over there
they disembark
and in their hearts
they start to quake

they march and march
oh christ i'm sore
and at the front
they march no more

their cause is great
their cause is just
gods on their side
he's british right

the enemy
where is he      there!
he's near enough
to share a jar

how are you hun
what's cooking boche
its killing time
i'm sorry son

the trenches stink
the bodies rot
in no mans land
oh what a war

dear mam and dad
i'm feeling great
wish you were here
oh no I don't

the mad moiselles
are willing but
they give you pox
our noses rot

jack's lost an arm
bill's lost his head
i'm still alive
or am I dead

the home fires burn
back there in blighty
in god we trust
fuck you almighty

if only i
you bloody cant
i want to sleep
just shift your arse

over the top
you stumble on
strung on barbed wire
you cry for mam

he did his duty
manfully
he died to keep
the empire free

the bugle sounds
its over now
in flanders fields
the poppies grow

# War Photographer

The pictures must be right. Close
enough to see the corpse but not
the face sliced half away
the gut spilling out.

# Gear Change

Birds drop off trees
with hunger. Fish shrink
to fin and bone.  Cats
caterwaul.  Dogs
wolf humans down.

No-one has seen it coming.
Carbon footprints don't figure.
Don't blame The Bomb.
Don't blame anything.

The end of things
had to be like this,
as unexpected
as the beginning.

The Big Bang
in reverse
is merely
a change of gear.

# Talking

Empty chairs.  I talk to them sometimes,
knowing they won't reply.  I tell them
what I've been doing, where I am going,
but nothing indecently slight.  When someone
sits in them they are still empty.
Of purpose, of meaning, of life.

# Moonglow

The moon shone dazzling-bright
with borrowed light.
So do we glow
with virtues of people we know.

# Alltlwyd

birdsong insinuates
into the light
trees lattice
the new sky
colour
is not yet
it will come
like thought
cloaking
elementals

# Buttered Bun

She would take me to the café
for elevenses
though we didn't call it that.

I was fourteen.
She was my sister.

*We'll have a buttered bun,*
she said, smiling,
*And a coffee of course.*

The buttered bun
was delicious.
A treat like no other.

Since then I have had
buns with butter
but nothing quite like this.

It was a thing
exactly of its time
just like herself.

# Birds

Far to the right – up there, up there! –
I see birds flying. They are dark,
impenetrable, like the thoughts
of alabaster virgins. Take me
or not, they say. There is nothing
we can do but savour them.

# Shadows

Over and above the wreck
of undistinguished dreams I find
shadows on walls long gone.
My sisters make them, curling
fingers into shapes
of beasts and flowers I know
or can imagine.
They cannot tell
that one day I will see those shapes again
when they are shadowless.

# Fields

Beyond the touch
and wreck of thoughts
lie fields of unperception.
Simply they are.

# Tears

Tears come hard
after our infancy

but age
softens us

they flow like wine.

# Death

The chill of Lilian's death
affects all nature. Since she died
the planet has turned white.
We see it in the photographs
from space that can't be argued with.
All steadiness has gone. We dare
not go outdoors. All this
has come about because of her.

# Religiously

Do you write each day
religiously? he asked.
What could I say?
No, not quite religiously,
more agnostically,
questioning everything,
clauses and sub-clauses,
parentheses, commas,
even the random semi-colon.
If once I wrote religiously,
where would it end?
I might emerge a bishop
sermonising in *The Times*,
or a monk avoiding women
like the plague they seldom are.

I could even make a killing
of myself and other people.

A godless thing, this writing,
thank the Lord.

# Choices

Sick of the lies, the pain, the self-
questioning, one thinks
of various possibilities. Hanging
is too crude, too taut
with doubt. How long until
unconsciousness; how black
the time before? Choking's
not for me, tongue
livid, feet
kicking at air.

And then there's drowning.
A kindly death, some say,
after the last gasp, brain
crying fool. But what
lung-bursting first,
and the mess you leave on the beach,
for someone to find
while walking the dog, or contemplating
the divine inscrutability of nature.

Being hit by a train
means instant death
unless one simply has one's legs
slung over the line, but who
in their wrong mind would do that?
And surely the sight of the thing,
or the sound of it, if one's back
is cowardly turned
would make one leap aside,
too late perhaps?
To be left a slavering wreck
is hardly improvement.

Then there are the exotica:
jumping off cliffs,

trailing tubes from exhausts,
putting poison into one's ear
 (only for the avidly literary).
And saddest of all,
the popping of pills,
customary cry for help
of adolescent girls.

Perhaps the Romans had it right.
Falling on one's sword
is swift, manly and certain.
So long as the sword doesn't snap.

# Truisms

White does not always win, nor black deny.
The loudest noise can go unheard.
Strange is but relative.
True hearts are false to those
they used to love.

# Pillars

Greasy pillars of something like lard
get lodged in odd places
like the hatbox Prince Philip wears
when he inspects the troops in Honduras.

Or the physical means of escape
by drainpipe or sponge.

It all depends of course
on what you mean by sponge
as C.E.M. Joad used to say
on a Brains Trust programme I have long forgotten.

# Terry Hetherington

*1936-2007*

A worker's strength
In his prime

A poet's truth
For all time

# Prophecy

The leaves scratching the glass fulfil
an ancient prophecy:  that time
would not allow the house to rest.
Wind-breaths insinuate themselves
through locks and cracks.  Worms
butt their heads at doors.  Frost
bites. Rains rot. Snows
shiver as they slide.

People, feeling this, have stayed
here fitfully,
their brief, fragmented lives beset
by ills that chime
with all the house has known.